SUPERCROSS
BUMPS AND JUMPS

BY LISA J. AMSTUTZ

CAPSTONE PRESS
a capstone imprint

Published by Capstone Press, an imprint of Capstone
1710 Roe Crest Drive, North Mankato, Minnesota 56003
capstonepub.com

Copyright © 2026 by Capstone. All rights reserved. No part of this publication may be reproduced in whole or in part, or stored in a retrieval system, or transmitted in any form or by any means, electronic, mechanical, photocopying, recording, or otherwise, without written permission of the publisher.

Library of Congress Cataloging-in-Publication Data
Names: Amstutz, Lisa J., author.
Title: Supercross : bumps and jumps / by Lisa J. Amstutz.
Description: North Mankato, Minnesota : Capstone Press, [2026] | Series: Dirt bike blast | Includes bibliographical references and index. | Audience: Ages 9-11 | Audience: Grades 4-6 | Summary: "The crowd roars in the packed arena as the dirt bikes take off. The bikes fly high over a triple jump. They dash over a sand section and twist around corners. It's a fight to the finish, and only one rider will come out on top. Put readers in the center of the supercross action as they learn about everything from race rules to track features and equipment. Carefully leveled, high-energy text helps ensure accessibility for even the most reluctant readers"— Provided by publisher.
Identifiers: LCCN 2024054873 (print) | LCCN 2024054874 (ebook) | ISBN 9798875226175 (hardcover) | ISBN 9798875226120 (paperback) | ISBN 9798875226137 (pdf) | ISBN 9798875226144 (epub) | ISBN 9798875226151 (kindle edition)
Subjects: LCSH: Supercross—Juvenile literature. | Trail bikes—Juvenile literature.
Classification: LCC GV1060.1455 .A47 2026 (print) | LCC GV1060.1455 (ebook) | DDC 796.7/56—dc23/eng/20241220
LC record available at https://lccn.loc.gov/2024054873
LC ebook record available at https://lccn.loc.gov/2024054874

Editorial Credits
Editor: Carrie Sheely; Designer: Dina Her; Media Researcher: Donna Metcalf; Production Specialist: Tori Abraham

Image Credits
Alamy: Anne-Marie Sorvin/Sipa USA, 16, 19, 27; Associated Press: Jeff Roberson, 15; Getty Images: Gary Newkirk/ALLSPORT, 29, Baptiste Fernandez/Icon Sport, 28, Christian Petersen, 20, Genaro Molina/Los Angeles Times, 13, Will Lester/MediaNews Group/Inland Valley Daily Bulletin, 8, 25; Newscom: Anne-Marie Sorvin/Sipa USA, 4-5, Panoramic/ZUMAPRESS, 18, 23; Shutterstock: Artur Didyk, cover, 7, 11, Diego Barbieri, 14, Dave Hewison Photography, 21, 24, EvrenKalinbacak, 17

Design Elements
Shutterstock: backup, Goromaru, JACKREZNOR, Miloje, salam kerrong

Any additional websites and resources referenced in this book are not maintained, authorized, or sponsored by Capstone. All product and company names are trademarks™ or registered® trademarks of their respective holders.

Printed and bound in China. 006276

TABLE OF CONTENTS

All About Supercross 6

Getting Ready 12

Race Time! 18

Going Pro 26

    Glossary 30

    Read More 31

    Internet Sites 31

    Index 32

    About the Author 32

> Words in **bold** are in the glossary.

WHAT IS SUPERCROSS?

Supercross is an exciting dirt bike race on a dirt track. It is held in a stadium.

knobby tires

disc brake cover

SUPERCROSS BIKE DIAGRAM

stiff suspension

powerful engine

CHAPTER 1
ALL ABOUT SUPERCROSS

It's supercross time! Fans pack the stadium. A dirt track is set up inside. It is short and **narrow**. There is not much space. Racers weave around tight turns and fly over jumps. They fight to keep the lead.

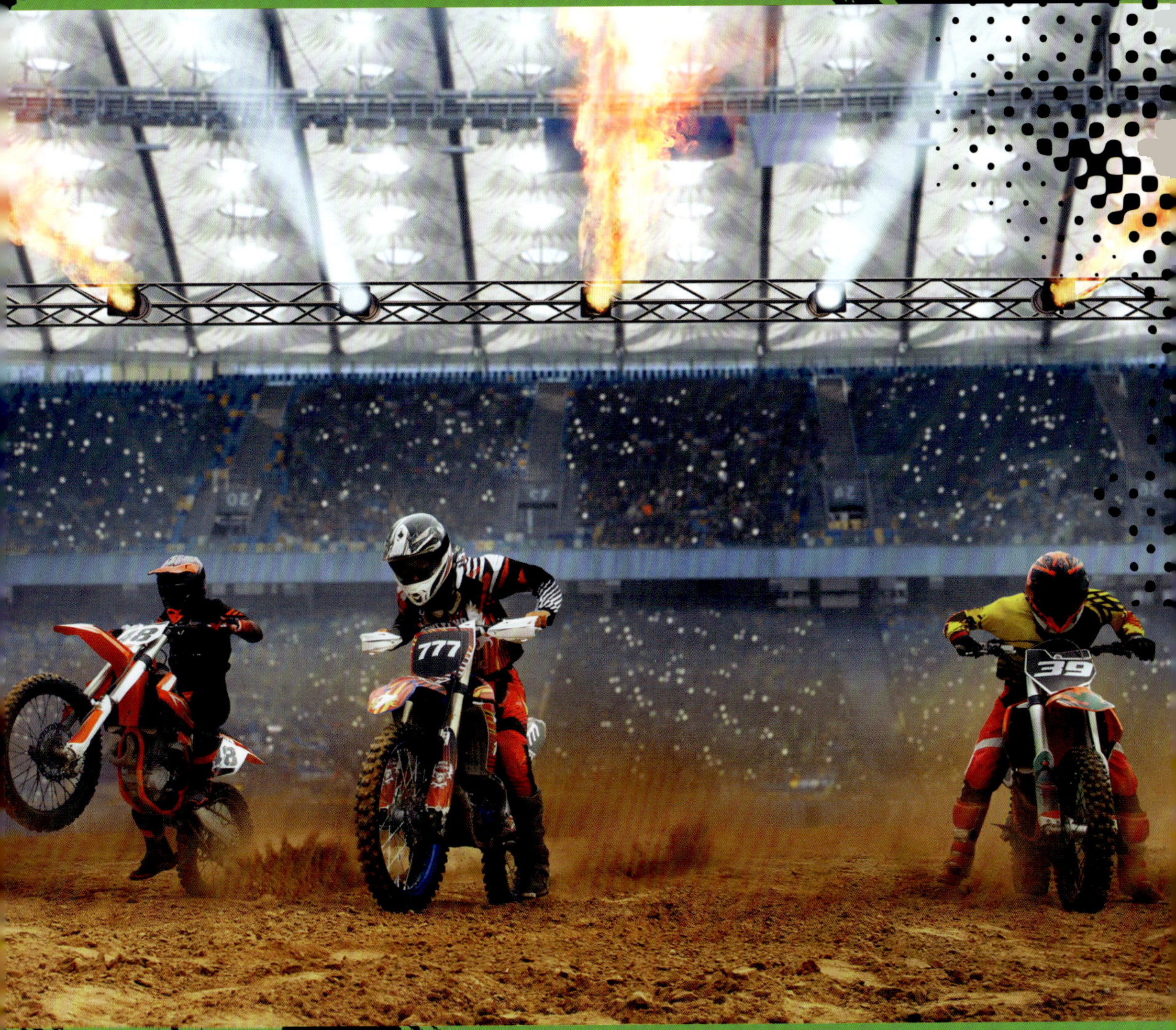
777
39

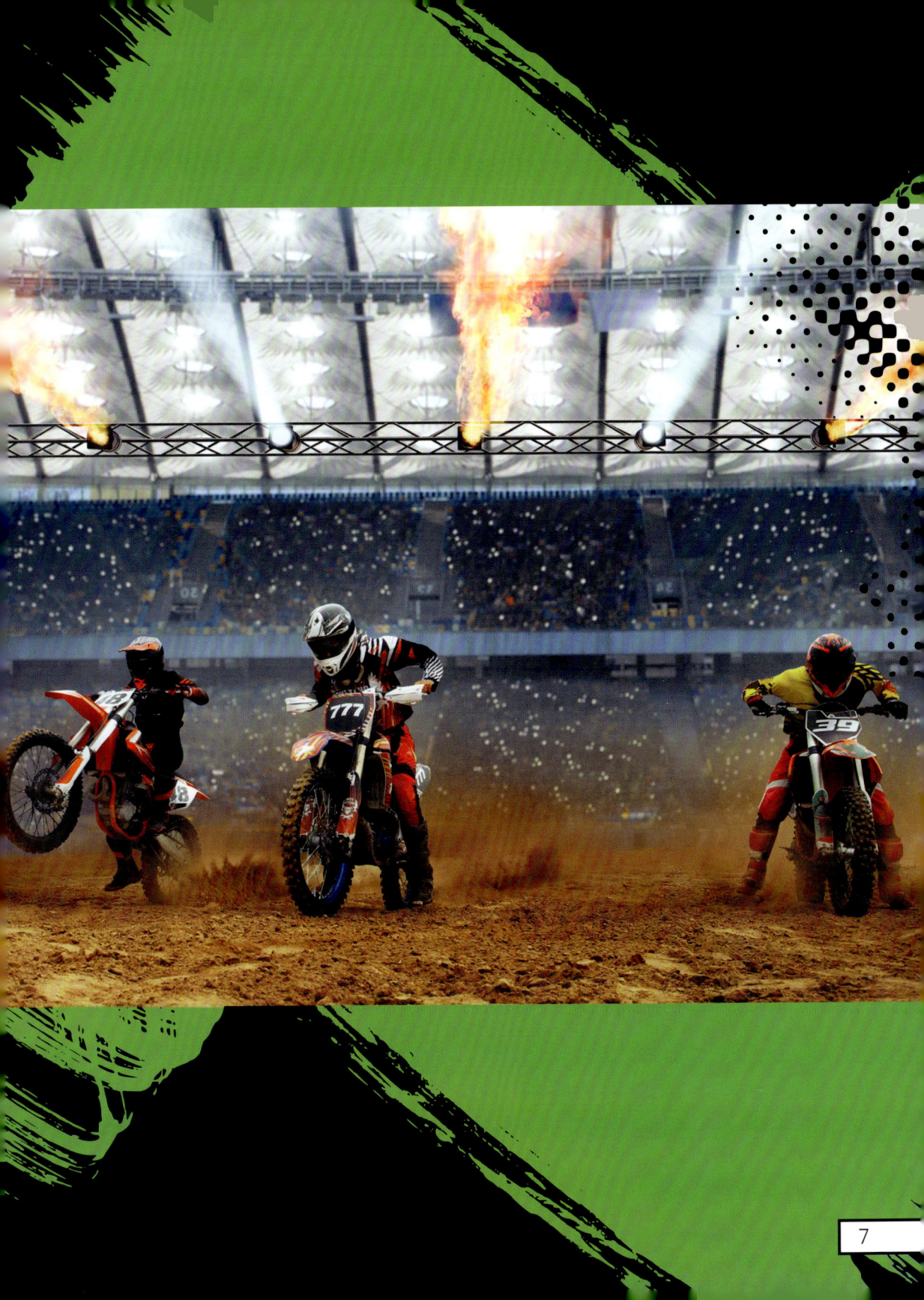

A rider does a celebratory move after winning an AMA Supercross Championship race.

The first supercross race was held in 1972. It was called the Superbowl of Motocross. By 1976, the event name was changed to supercross.

Now events are held all over the world. One of the biggest U.S. **series** is the American Motorcyclist Association (AMA) Supercross Championship.

Supercross races have different classes. Some are based on the type of bike engine. Some classes for **amateurs** are based on the riders' ages.

FACT

Many supercross riders also race motocross. Motocross races have similar but larger courses outdoors.

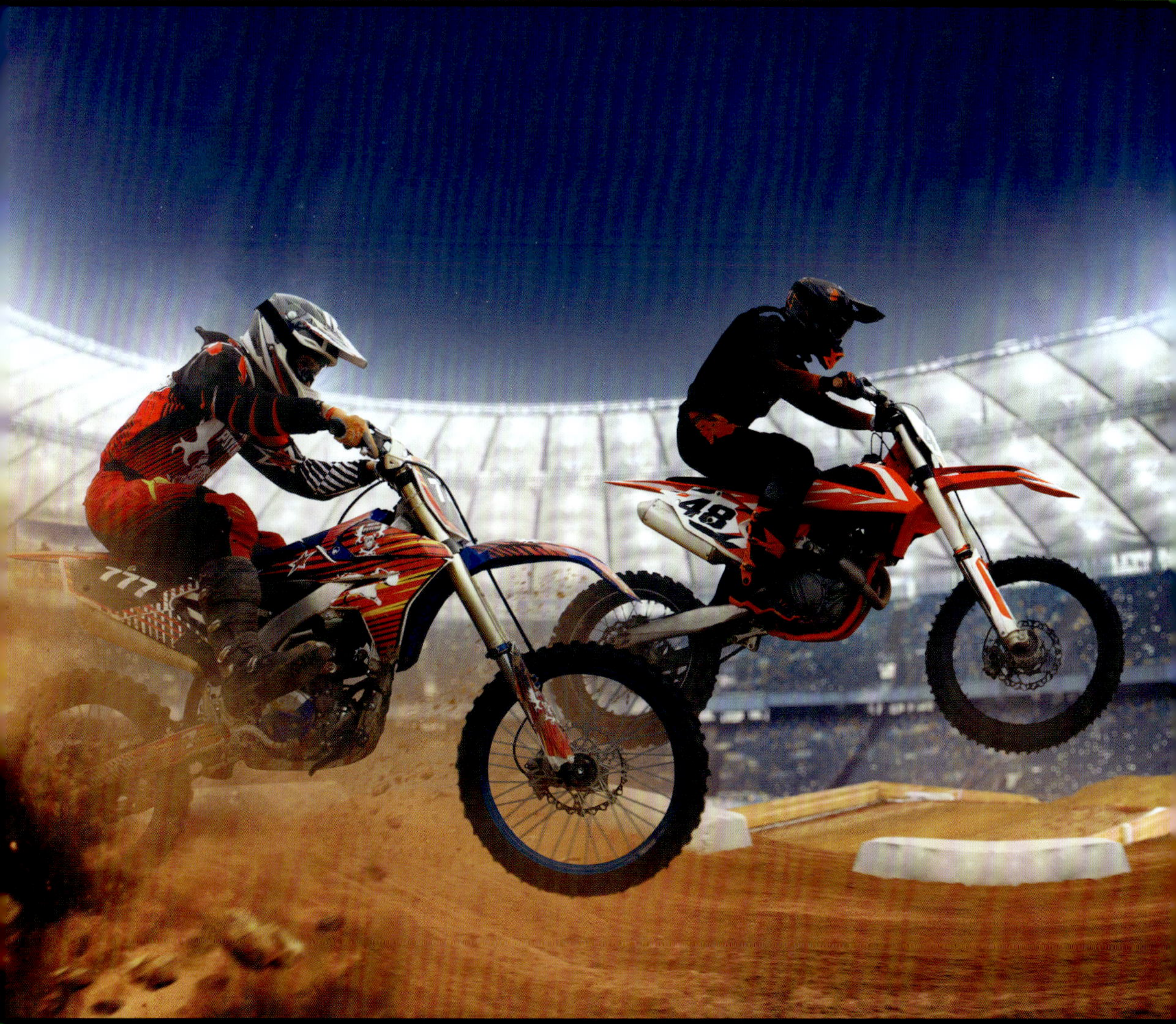
777
48

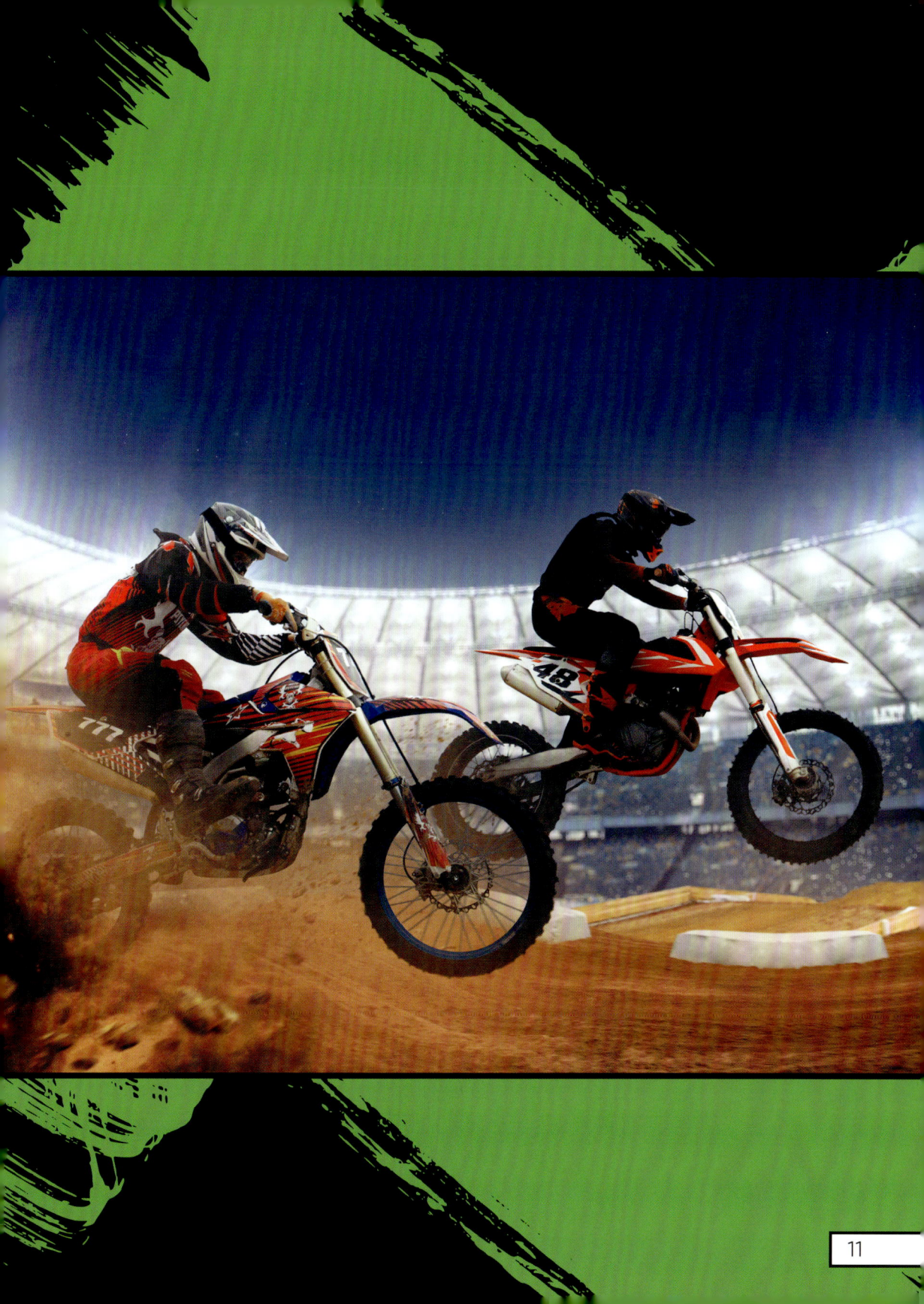

CHAPTER 2
GETTING READY

Scoop! Dump! Pack! The set-up crew lays more than 5,000 sheets of wood or plastic in the stadium. Dump trucks haul in load after load of dirt. The first layer is packed down. The rest is shaped into a **course**.

FACT
The dirt in a supercross course weighs about 26 million pounds (12 million kilograms)!

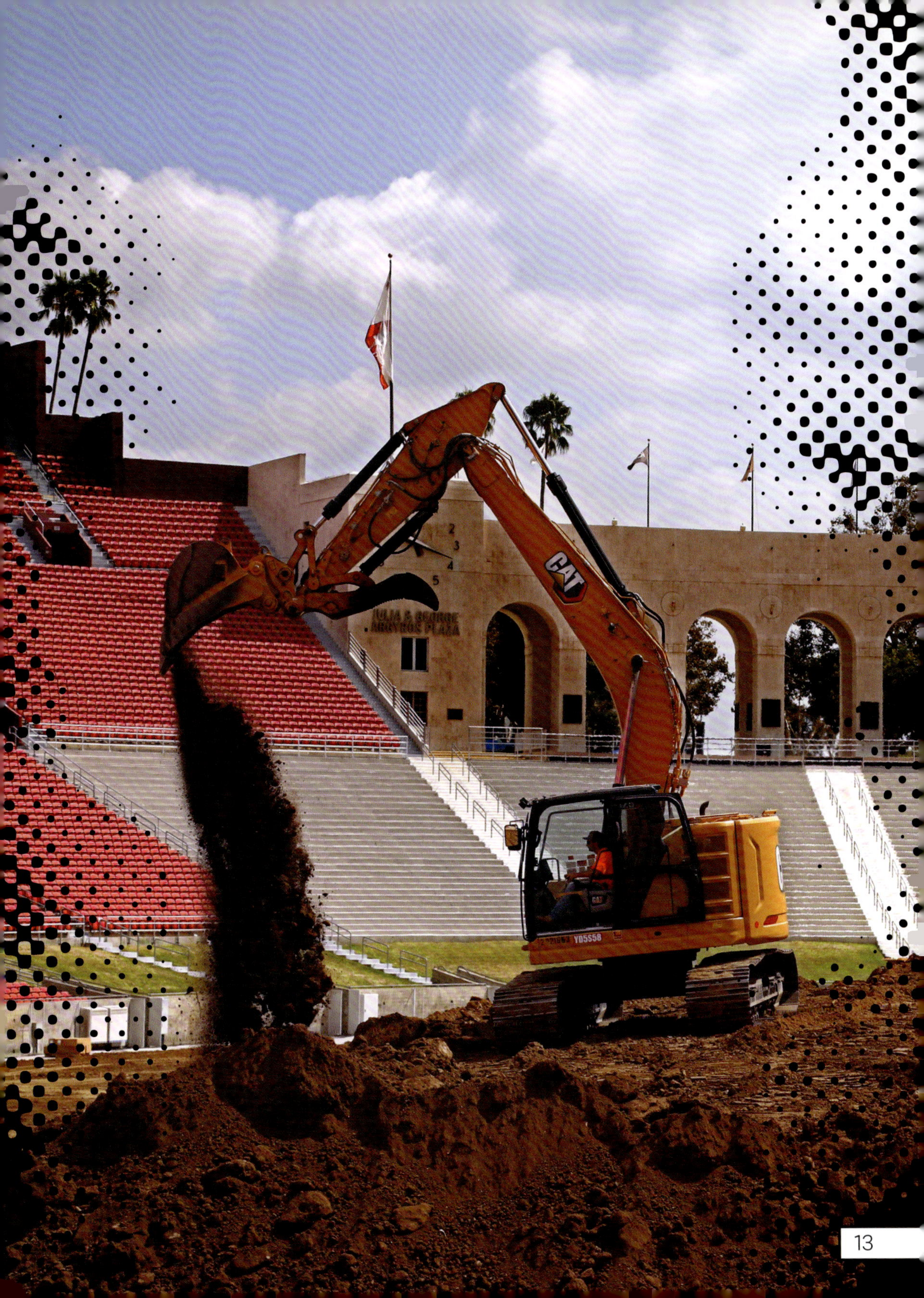
CAT

The machines form bumps, turns, and jumps. Whoops are a string of small bumps. Each is about 3 feet (0.9 m) tall. Riders try to skim over the top. A dragon's back rises and ends with a small jump.

A supercross course in Italy

Riders race over whoops.

FACT

The rider leading the AMA Supercross Championship series has a red plate on their bike. This makes it easy to find the top scorer.

15

A supercross course is tough! Riding it takes strength and skill. Racers train hard. They lift weights. They might run, bike, and swim. They spend hours practicing. They choose healthy foods.

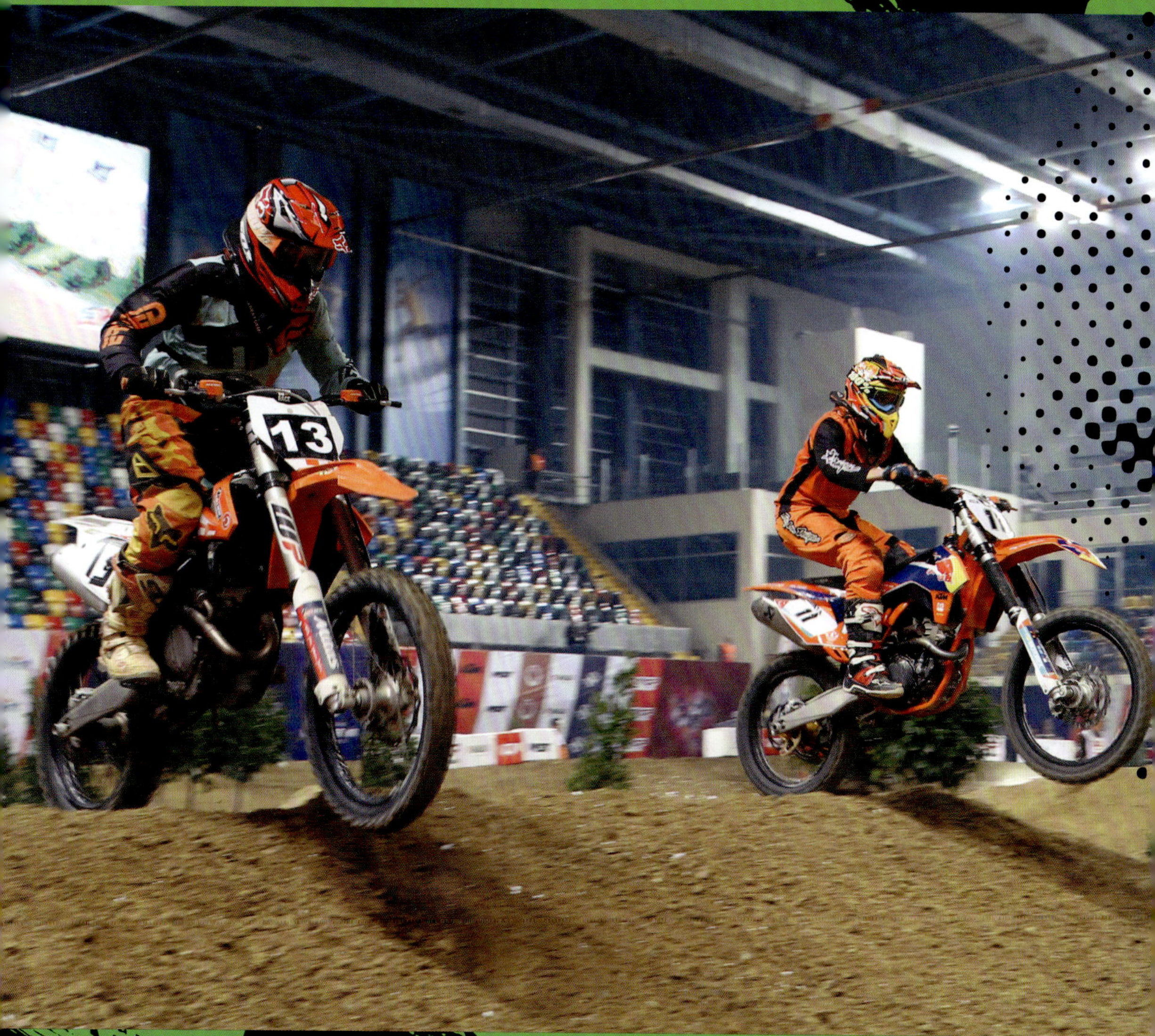
13

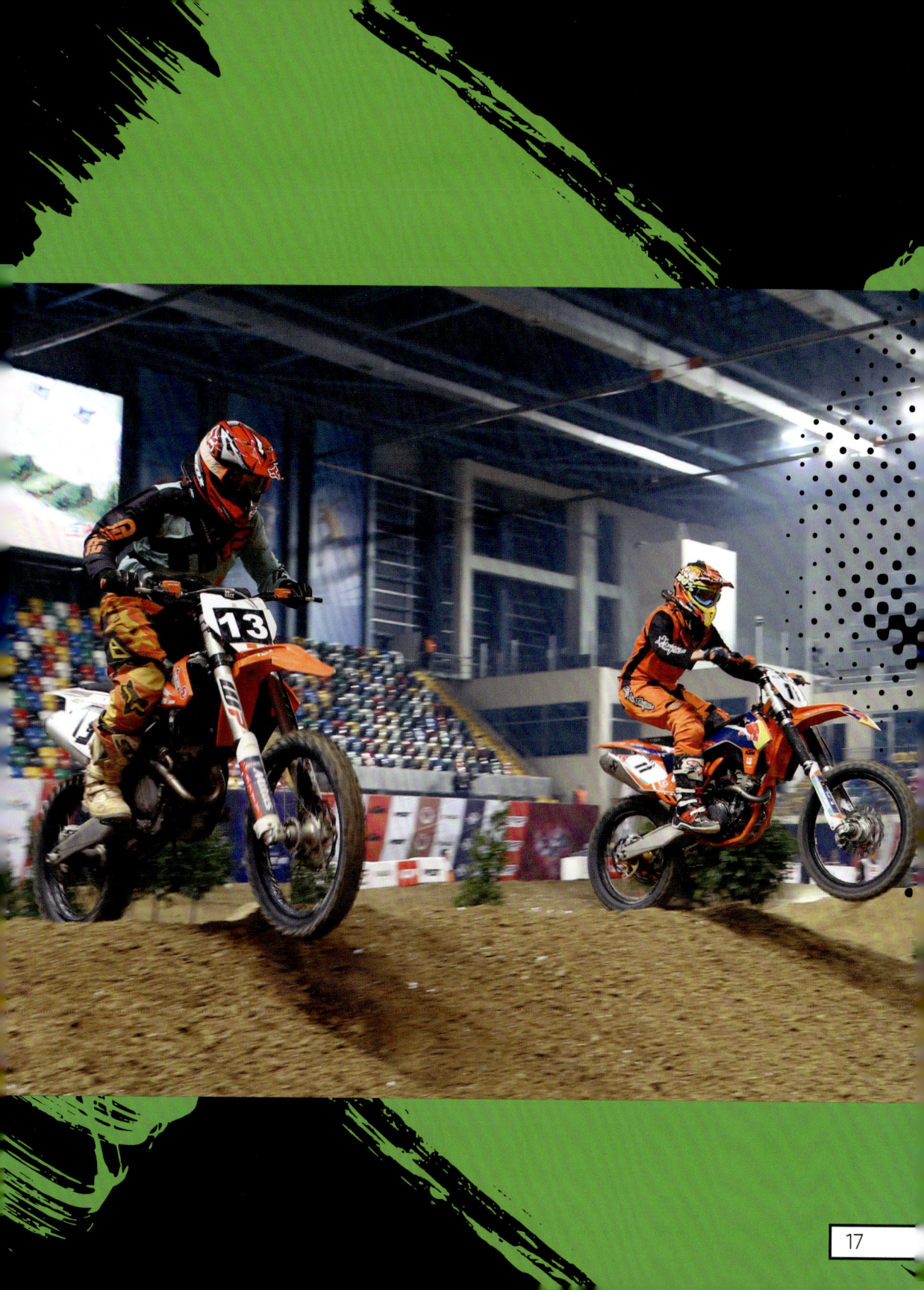

CHAPTER 3
RACE TIME!

Race day is here! The riders suit up. They wear safety gear. It includes suits with body armor. Riders wear gloves, boots, and goggles. A helmet protects a rider's head.

In the AMA Supercross Championship series, practice rounds come first. These are timed races. The top riders in each class will move on. Then it's time for the **heat** races.

Riders with the best times will be in the **main event**. They get the best starting spots. The other riders have one more chance to get into the main event. They race in the last chance qualifier.

At last, it's time for the main event! The stadium lights come on. The top racers line up at the starting line. They rev their engines. *Vroom!*

The gate drops. And they're off! Here comes the first turn! Each racer tries to get the **hole shot**. The riders lean in as the crowd roars.

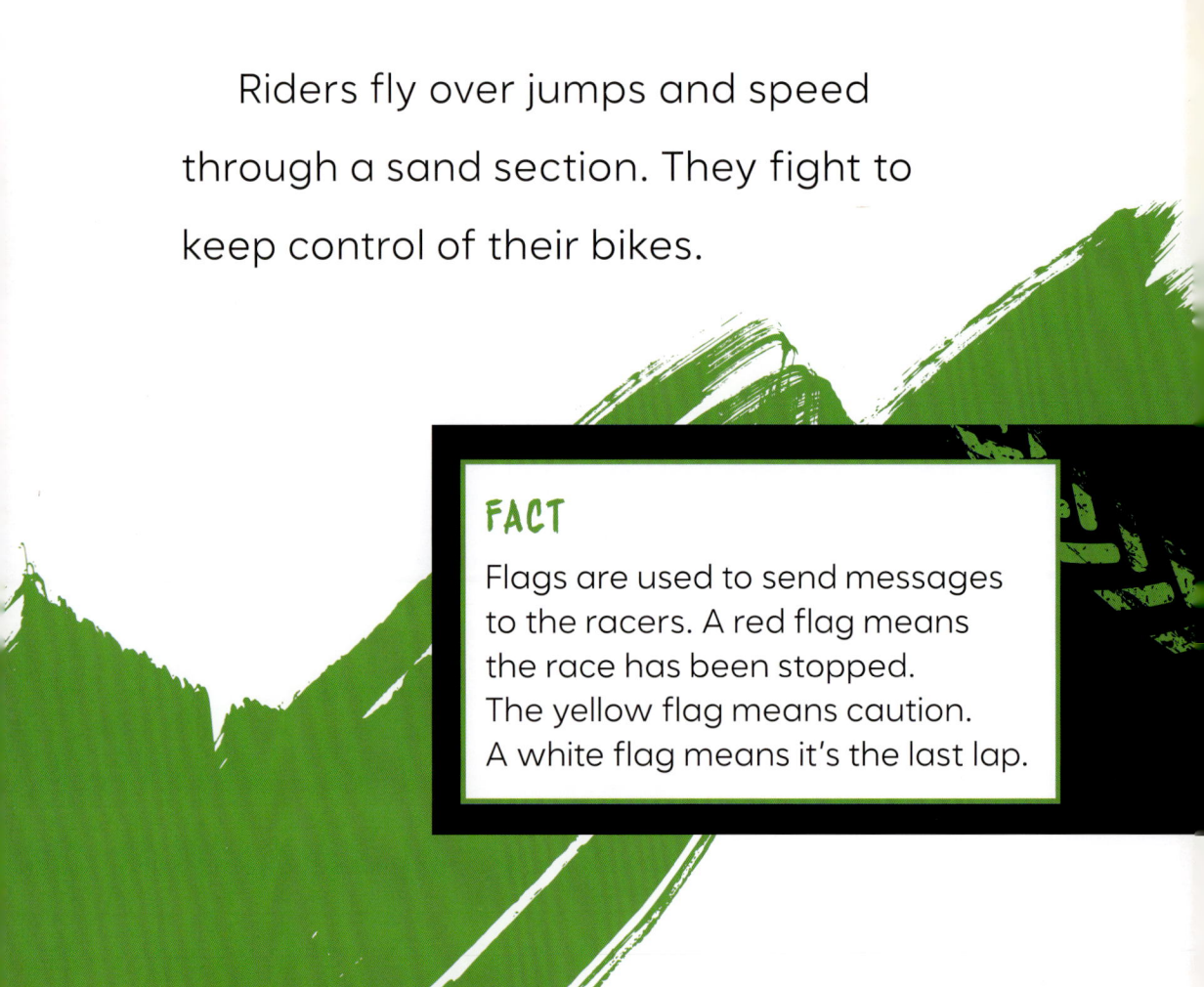

Riders fly over jumps and speed through a sand section. They fight to keep control of their bikes.

FACT

Flags are used to send messages to the racers. A red flag means the race has been stopped. The yellow flag means caution. A white flag means it's the last lap.

Racers take off from the starting line.

Soon riders face a triple jump! They launch into the air and land on the downslope of the third jump. Some soar 35 feet (11 m) high. That's about as high as a three-story building!

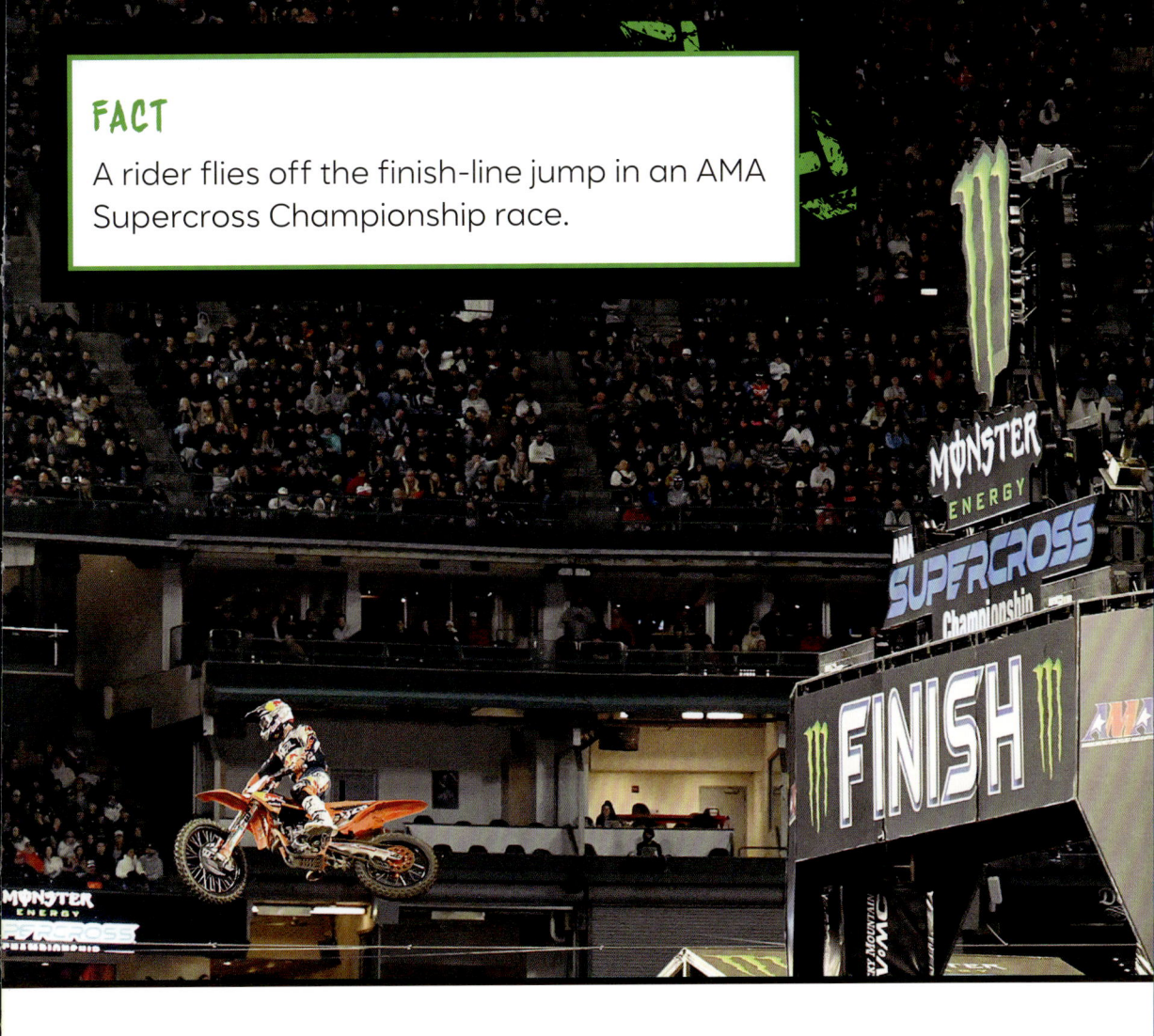

> **FACT**
> A rider flies off the finish-line jump in an AMA Supercross Championship race.

Crash! A rider goes off the course. The rest speed on. At last, they reach the finish line. The checkered flag waves. The winners stand on the **podium**.

CHAPTER 4
GOING PRO

Fans pack stadiums to see professional supercross racers. The AMA Supercross Championship has 17 races. Pros from around the world compete in the World Supercross Championship.

Vince Friese competes in the World Supercross Championship.

Fans keep a close eye on supercross stars. One of these is Cooper Webb. Born in 1996, he started racing at age 4. He has won two AMA Supercross Championships.

Cooper Webb

Jeremy McGrath

Jeremy McGrath is known as the King of Supercross. He won the AMA Supercross Championship seven times. He won the World Supercross Championship twice. Who will be the next superstar?

GLOSSARY

amateur (AM-uh-chur)—an athlete who takes part in a sport for pleasure rather than for money

course (KORS)—a route that racers follow

heat (HEET)—one of several races where the outcome helps decide who will advance to the main event

hole shot (HOL SHOT)—when a racer leads around the first turn of a supercross race

main event (MAYN i-VENT)—the final race in a supercross event

narrow (NA-roh)—not wide

podium (POH-dee-uhm)—a platform where winners receive their prizes

series (SERE-eez)—several events that people compete in that lead to an overall series champion

READ MORE

Abdo, Kenny. *Motocross*. Minneapolis: Abdo Zoom, 2024.

Conaghan, Bernard. *Motocross*. New York: Crabtree Publishing, 2023.

Golusky, Jackie. *Supercross: Rev It Up!* Minneapolis: Lerner Publications, 2023.

INTERNET SITES

AMA Supercross
americanmotorcyclist.com/racing/professional-racing/ama-supercross

Motorsports Hall of Fame of America: Jeremy McGrath
mshf.com/hall-of-fame/inductees/jeremy-mcgrath.html

World Supercross Championship
wsxchampionship.com

INDEX

AMA Supercross
   Championship, 9, 15,
   19, 26, 28, 29

classes, 10
course setup, 12

dragon's back, 14

flags, 22, 25

hole shot, 22

jumps, 6, 14, 22, 24, 25

main events, 20, 21
McGrath, Jeremy, 29

podiums, 25

safety gear, 18
Superbowl of
   Motocross, 9

training, 16

Webb, Cooper, 28
whoops, 14
World Supercross
   Championship, 26,
   27, 29

ABOUT THE AUTHOR

Lisa J. Amstutz is the author of more than 150 children's books on topics ranging from applesauce to zebra mussels. An ecologist by training, she enjoys sharing her love of nature with kids. Lisa lives on a small farm with her family.